To the Buzzer

To the Buzzer

BRIAN L. TUCKER

RESOURCE *Publications* • Eugene, Oregon

TO THE BUZZER

Copyright © 2020 Brian L. Tucker. All rights reserved. Except for brief quotations in critical publications or reviews, no part of this book may be reproduced in any manner without prior written permission from the publisher. Write: Permissions, Wipf and Stock Publishers, 199 W. 8th Ave., Suite 3, Eugene, OR 97401.

Resource Publications
An Imprint of Wipf and Stock Publishers
199 W. 8th Ave., Suite 3
Eugene, OR 97401

www.wipfandstock.com

PAPERBACK ISBN: 978-1-7252-8469-2
HARDCOVER ISBN: 978-1-7252-8470-8
EBOOK ISBN: 978-1-7252-8471-5

Manufactured in the U.S.A. 10/05/20

For Harrison, who taught me the game.

The invention of basketball was not an accident. It was developed to meet a need. Those boys simply would not play "Drop the Handkerchief."

—James Naismith

CONTENTS

Acknowledgments | ix

Inventions | 1
#42 | 2
Numbers | 3
Michael, No Relation | 4
Color | 5
Supper | 6
Pine Pony | 7
Bobcat | 8
Conditioning | 10
Open Gym | 11
Hack-a-Shaq | 13
Intestinal Fortitude | 14
Roll Call | 15
Height | 16
You wanna be the best... | 17
Scouts | 18
Lace Up Those Nikes | 19
Housing Aussies | 20
Outlet Passes | 21
Mom | 22
Single A | 23
Thumped | 25
Video Games | 26
Home | 27
Isis Dupree | 28
Game Night | 29

Denim | 30
Air Ball | 32
Ball Hog | 33
9-2 | 35
Ring-Ring-Ring | 37
Playlist | 38
Dunk You, Very Much | 39
Bank Shot (The Bank is OPEN) | 41
10-3 | 42
Water Break | 43
Block Party | 44
Big City | 47
Technical | 50
Tonic-Clonic Seizures | 52
Post Up (Box Out) | 54
Chocolate Milk | 55
Game Night Again | 58
Visit | 60
Rally Hats | 61
Free Weights | 64
Quintuple-Double | 66
Run-and-Gun | 68
Four High | 71
Scouts | 73
Pick and Roll | 75
Decisions | 77
Defensive Shift | 78

Lunch | 79
Healthy | 81
Bump | 83
Physical | 86
Heroes | 88
Basketball/Love | 89
No Pain No Gain | 90
SUPERvision | 93
Promises | 95
Ball Don't Lie | 96
Double Dribble | 97
This is War | 100
Xs and Os | 103
Zoo Keepers | 107
Isolation | 110

Fast break | 112
Shooting Range | 113
Best Friend | 115
Basketball Blues | 118
ESPN Recruiting | 121
Rest | 125
Repaired | 126
Ghost | 129
Swimming | 130
Seton Herald | 134
Stalwart | 136
Memorial | 137
Perseverance | 138
The Current Game
  of Basketball | 140

ACKNOWLEDGMENTS

In addition to Harrison's legacy, this book is the result of experiences at Monticello Independent School: the best school in the history of public education. R.I.P. my beloved, independent school. Trojan pride forever! Also, I wouldn't be typing words without my professors and peers at Bluegrass Writers Studio. And I'm extremely grateful to the staff at Wipf and Stock for bringing this book to your eyes. Big thanks to Emily Calvanese for bringing the characters to life with her art skills.

INVENTIONS

Dr. James Naismith invented basketball　　　　in 1892.
Coach said he was *ahead*　　　　　　　　　　*of his time.*
The game looked way different back　　　　　then.
Three straight fouls from one opponent meant　a goal for the other.
A five second call on an in-bounds play meant　a foul, not a turnover.
The game was two fifteen-minute halves,　　　with a five-minute breather.

I wondered what made them change so much.
Who dunked first?
Why was dunking illegal at one point?
Who killed it, besides MJ, Kobe, and LeBron?
Would my best friend, Mike, one day play in the NBA?
Would he remember me in Seton, Kentucky?

#42

I didn't pick the number so much as *it*
picked ME.

Jackie Robinson wore it, too.
He was THE G.O.A.T.

But *that* was baseball
and THIS . . .
is basketball.

The ball is bigger
than me.

It's the dopest game
in the world.

NUMBERS

are usually smaller
for shooting guards
like one, two, three
and
twenty-three
like Michael Jordan.

I wanted to be
like MJ.
So did everyone else at
Seton Middle
where me and Mike
went to school.

MICHAEL, NO RELATION

He wasn't #23 of the Chicago Bulls
but Mike Mulaney of Highway 47,

just north of town
and a few blocks past
Smitty's fast-food joint.

He wanted to be a shooting guard, too,
but his hand gave him more bricks
than a mansion-sized home.

He laughed with me
and took it on the chin.

He was seven-feet tall,
and so at center was where he stood.

COLOR

shouldn't be
a big deal
off the court.

But it was.

People stared at
Mike like he was an
enigma, a mystery.

He was darker than most
folks in Seton and
one time he even ran home, he said.

I didn't stare at him 'cuz
he was my friend
and that was stronger

than blood,

or, any dumb

racist.

SUPPER

Mom made the best
country cooking
and Mike said, *Thanks.*
The corn bread and
pinto beans swam in
soup.
I wanted to tell Mom about the
stares Mike got, but I
didn't.
The ladle fetched more
soup like
she knew better
than to ruin the meal.

PINE PONY

*You won't find me
on the bench this year*, I said.
My days on the pine pony are done.

*Let's just see your jump shot go THROUGH
the net, bruh,* Mike teased, throwing the ball my way,
setting an imaginary screen on no one.

I lined my toes up and shot with
confidence.

The net *SWISHED* sweet music,

and Mike said, *Eww wee that's sic, Bobcat.*

BOBCAT

stuck as a nickname.

It didn't hurt that it was my ALL-TIME favorite
animal.

I loved how they lurked in the woods
behind my home.

Sometimes I thought I saw them,
but usually it was a rabbit or fox.

Coach one time said, *You're moving like a bobcat out there,
Levi,* and the rest was history.

Mike got the whole Seton team to chime in.
Before I knew it, it was,
Bobcat this and
Hey, Bobcat, shoot the rock!

CONDITIONING

We climbed "the ladder"
as Coach called it—
to HEAVEN!
And when that wasn't high enough,
we went back to the
start.

Climbing the ladder was
one sprint down the court
with four seconds on the clock.

Then, we went down and back
with seven seconds.

And down-back-down at only
eleven seconds.

It was the worst, even though
we knew it made us stronger.

Coach blew the whistle even when one player
didn't cross the line in time,
before the buzzer sounded.

Ozzie puked in a five-gallon trashcan.
Cade grabbed his side and struggled to
breathe.

Mike looked over at me and said only what Mike would,

Is that all he's got?

OPEN GYM

was better.

We played pick-up games

and didn't worry about much.

Mike didn't anyways.

I worked on my FUN-damentals

to be game ready.

Mike slammed the ball so hard through the rim

sparks flew off the orange metal.

DANG, Mike! Ozzie hooted.

I thought of Shaquille O' Neal

as he skied for lob after lob

on old YouTube videos.

HACK-A-SHAQ

It was a term we'd loved   ever since
first hearing it   on TV,
and I said it over and over again   to Mike,
as he stepped to the foul line,   trying to not brick another,
only to hear *CLANK*,   watching the ball ricochet
far FAR, away into the   bleachers.

INTESTINAL FORTITUDE

Coach told us that's what we had—
intestinal fortitude.

He was reading some big books at the time.
Some with over three-hundred pages.
There weren't any pictures inside *those* books.
(Mike snuck a peek when Coach went to the can
one day.)

Not a single picture.

Hey, Bobcat. What's he mean with this 'infestinal tortitude' crap?

*It means don't be a sus, and
we'll win every game.*

Sounds like a disease.

Probably is, I said, with a smile.

ROLL CALL

We hyped ourselves up after
endless puking
and leg cramps from "the ladder"
and told ourselves it was ALL
worth it.

When we weren't listening to old-school Biggie,
lifting weights
in the locker room,
we chanted made-up lyrics.

Mike would shout,

His name is Bobcat.

And everyone would shout

Yeah

He likes to fight

Yeah

So when you see him hit

Yeah

You know he's lit.

And the song would make its way around
and arrive back to Mike,
who always spit the best verses
imaginable.

HEIGHT

I was only 5' 10" and that was *after*
a growth spurt.

The word 'spurt' made me laugh.
We started calling everything
'spurt.'

On the bus, the ball boy
called Coach that, trying to be
funny.

What'd you say, kid?

Nuh . . . nuhthin', Coach, he squeaked.

We all roared.
We won that night and were 4-0 for the first time
in a loooooong time.
A rare feat for Seton JVers.

YOU WANNA BE THE BEST . . .

You gotta beat the best, Coach said. *This is a lesson in humility, gentlemen.*

We didn't have a clue what his big books
were teaching him now, and we didn't have time to ask.

Bursting through the gym doors,
came the varsity Seton girls squad,
basketballs-in-hand.

My mouth actually dropped,
and I checked my jersey to make sure it
was tucked all the way into my shorts.

Ozzie swallowed his gum.
Mike looked sideways at me.

This scrimmage was BRUTAL.

Seton's best girl shooter
guarded me.
And she shut me down.
I couldn't buy a bucket, and
she didn't give an inch.

The few times I accidentally
brushed the ball with my hand,
she quickly went into a triple-threat
pose and taunted me to take
HER BALL AWAY.

The girls beat us in three straight games,
and Mike didn't dunk once.

SCOUTS

After the beat down from the girls . . .
It was odd   but fun.
Mike was a phenom   that year.
Scouts came to see *him*   from all over.
And I tossed alley-oop after oop   to him.
And he launched himself like a rocket   skyward.
And the ball found the hoop, each time   like a magnet.
And the crowd went wild, home and away   for us, him mainly.
And pencils scraped on the paper while   the goal wobbled wobbled
WOBBLED.

LACE UP THOSE NIKES

Mike wore his MJ shorts 24/7—
Carolina blue, his only color.
I was a UK fan,
and told him that's where he needed to go.
He waved me off like a fly.

I don't think so, Bobcat.

Don't you want to be your own superstar?

I do, but I'm chasing the best.

Why not go to one of those MJ camps then?

He held up his thumb and index finger and rubbed them together.

I don't have that kind of cash, do you?

We could go to Coach Cal's house. Put on a clinic for free.

Mike paused, dribbling the ball on the park's
worn asphalt.

We could. I do like FREE.

Kentucky blue is sweeter anyway, I reminded.

HOUSING AUSSIES

The Aussies came mid-season,
part of a winter tournament
in Seton.

They were placed with us,
in our homes if we had room.

The game of basketball
lost priority
the moment
one of the blokes said,
*Mate, we didn't come here for hoops. . .
we came for the cheerleaders.*

FYI: My sister was a cheerleader.
So, I balled up my fists in preparation for a
fight.

Mike said, *Let it go,
things are different down undah.*

I puffed out my chest
and was about to speak, when
a boomerang was given to me as a gift,
and I lost my spunk.

I tried to imagine what it was like
on the other side of the world
where boomerangs existed.

OUTLET PASSES

were   the best.
                                   Tossing the ball
                                 high off the backboard
                         and hearing the *thunk* as the ball
arced down   and I jumped up. It was a moment of
                 awesomeness. Mike running down court
           soaring to catch my pass
feeling the backboard *shake* like a snare drum.
Mike coming back to earth and the whole gym
GAWKING.

MOM

played
H-O-R-S-E
with me
in the backyard
after the Aussies left.

She always won, because
she thought about her shots
beforehand.

She held the leather ball
centered in her hand,
only her fingers touching it,
and spun it a few times
before taking aim.

She looked like a hunter
sighting a deer in the woods.

She lined up her body with the rim.
She put her right foot slightly more forward
than her left and
liftoff—
she rose with the ball
and let it spin, with backward
rotation
holding her hand up with the perfect,
manicured follow through, until
the ball dropped happily through
the hoop.
FYI: She used to play
ball at the University of Kentucky.

SINGLE A

Seton was tiny in
size.

We only had forty-eight people in our
eighth grade class.

We were too small to even field a football squad.

Too poor to boot, Coach muttered under his breath, when it was mentioned.

So we stuck with hoops.
It was easiest, because it could happen
anywhere.

A pick-up game could start with two: one-on-one
grow to four: two-on-two
then six: three-on-three
maybe eight: four-on-four
and with the magic number, ten: we could play five-on-five, until the janitor
told us to go home.

It came with the best price tag imaginable:
free.

THUMPED

We got beat-downs (and Varsity squad, too) from the larger, neighboring county schools.
Even with Mike Mulaney, we were still far from MJ's '92 Dream Team. We didn't have a Magic, a Pippen, or a Bird. We had four decent players, yours truly included, and Willie, our point guard. We were usually winded eight minutes into play. Coach called timeouts as much for our stamina as he did for the sic runs other, bigger schools would make.

Take a seat, he'd say, pointing to the bench.

Sometimes the ball boys would fill our jugs with Powerade instead of water—
a wicked treat.

Mike would look over at me and *thump* his chest.

Shoot it, Bobcat, he'd say.

I would hold my fist up to the group of JV huddled,
and we'd chant, *One, two, three, Seton!*

We'd break formation, and I'd look for the kick after
a simple V-cut inside the three and back out.

When it went *ring* through the net, barely scraping the back of the iron hoop,
the crowd would cheer, and we'd think about the cold Powerade,
sitting in the sideline cooler.

VIDEO GAMES

When Mike and me weren't talking hoops
or shooting hoops
we were playing NBA Street on Dad's old Playstation
letting our minds run wild.

We never said, *That can't happen*, or,
He traveled with the ball.

Instead, we took those moves to
heart, and we imagined what they'd look like
on Seton's court.

One of my favorites was the 'slip-and-slide'—
a move where the point guard would
bring the ball up and
when double-teamed, he'd start
dribbling like mad.

With no help in the defense's trap, the point guard, or PG,
would put his back to one opponent and
going to the ground he'd spin move (ball still bouncing)
and come up again moving
through the defenders to the basket
only to throw up a wicked lob
and be slammed down by
Amare Stoudamire or someone.

We played the game so much, I actually thought I was Steve Nash in real life
sometimes.

HOME

I practiced most nights until the sun went down
and then the streetlight came on,
and I played until the bugs all but took
over the light.

Then, I'd hear Mom shout, *Supper, Levi! It's getting cold.*

I played my heart out on the cracked concrete, because I knew
Mike was at the park playing.

He already had a mustache growing
on his upper lip.

A real mustache.

I asked Mom if I could have a razor, too.

Just in case.

ISIS DUPREE

I saw her spying me from the lockers,
between Seton classes one day.

I thought she was trying to memorize *my*
locker combination.

I kept my MJ cards in there.
I didn't need *that* kind of attention.

Yo, dawg. Ms. Dupree is checkin' you out, Mike said, nudging me.

I batted him away, but
he wouldn't leave.

He stroked his mustache and laughed.

She cheers at all the games. I even saw her at an away game looking fly, he added.

Really?

Honest truth, Bobcat.

I felt better about my locker combo and my MJ cards,
but I wondered
what she wanted.

GAME NIGHT

I saw her in the stands at Perry County.
It was an away game.
I blinked twice.
She wore a denim jacket and
held her arms tight like she was cold.

I couldn't think straight and my first two threes
went *BONG* off the back rim.

Coach said, *Settle down.*

When the shots didn't fall, I
took the ball inside.
I ball faked to our PG, Willie, and
dished to our small forward, Ozzie. He
zipped the ball back to me on the wing, and
I spied Mike looming in the paint. I drove baseline
and both defenders collapsed on me.

Mike nodded his head upward like it was NBA Street
come to life.
Before I planned it, I tossed the ball sidearm, around
a Perry County player's head—up to the rim and
KABOOM! went the ball through the hoop.

Our small crowd went wild. We won 49-45 in the final
seconds. I saw Isis and wondered how she would get
home.

DENIM

Isis caught me before the bus cranked to life.
I lowered the awkward, half-window.
You played really tight tonight.
Mike elbowed me on the bus seat, trying to keep me from looking like a noob.
I'm happy you came.
Dad likes to watch you all play.
Ohh, he does, I said, thinking she didn't really want to be here at all.
I liked the game, too, she said, almost like she could read my thoughts.
Mike hooted from inside the bus.
How'd you get your name? I asked before I could stop myself. *I mean, I just think it's different is all. . .*
Ozzie held up his finger, pleading with me to STOP.
I mean, is it like the same as the terrorist group?
(What a dummy, I was!)
Instead of running away from the bus, she laughed. Then, she looked at the pavement.
No. It's not a terrorist thing.
Oh. I—I see. (But, I didn't.)
It was just bad timing, I guess.
Mike begged me to say something else, ANYTHING ELSE.
Well, I liked seeing you, I mumbled again.
Mike lifted the window up, trying to save me from myself.
I liked the game, she offered again. *She you at school?*
I held up the peace sign. (I actually held up the peace sign.) And, she laughed.
Well, bye.
C-ya.

AIR BALL

I awoke from a nightmare.

We were back from Perry County, and
I'd went to bed at 1 AM.
I didn't even shower, which was
gross now that I think about it.
But I thought of Isis, her denim.
I swore I could smell her, still standing
beside the bus.
I replayed my dumb comment about her name.
Way to win her over, I said to the walls of my bedroom.
Isis Isis ISIS.
I went back to sleep and thought of bunkers below
ground. I dodged land mines and confused Afghanistan
with southern Kentucky.

A girl stood in her jean jacket in the middle of
a war zone. I reached out to touch her just before my
alarm went off.

BALL HOG

At practice the next day, I shot the lights out.

The net was on fire. I imagined smoke coming off
the nylon.
Buckets dropped left and right.
Mike joked that they'd have to put the fire out later.
Cade Rainey got mad when I wouldn't finish a set play.
Coach told me to stop being a ball hog.
But he couldn't blow his whistle loud enough
to get me to stop.
I kept thinking Isis would walk in, and she'd spot me
mid-jumper. But she didn't, and five o'clock meant
time to go home.

9-2

Our only two losses were from county schools,
but Coach wasn't happy.

No excuses. Y'all should be 11-0.

The assistants nodded like whipped puppies.
Coach was still reading his big books.

He dribbled the worn, Spalding ball out to mid-court and fired a dagger right through the iron.
See that. I haven't practiced in years, and I can still do THAT.
What do you think Bell County is gonna do? They don't take days off. They'll watch our game film and be ready for us.

I didn't think too much about the two drops in our schedule. My only thought was *I didn't pass it to Mike enough.*

Mike said the same thing in the locker room after practice.

Get me the rock and I won't let us lose again, he smiled—his mustache spreading out like it had wings.

You admiring the stash? he asked, drying off the sweat from his face.

I tried to look away but wasn't quick enough.

Bobcat is checking out my stash, guys!

I gave him a little push, and Cade told me to work on my speed. Maybe we wouldn't get beat forty against Bell.

I started to ball my fists up, but Ozzie said we needed everyone. And he meant it. We were too small to be enemies.

I thought of Coach knocking down that shot. I knew he could hoop, but I'd never really thought about him *before* he was Coach.

RING-RING-RING

I picked up on the third ring with
sweaty palms.

Hey, a soft voice said.
Hey, I said, voice squeaking at the worst possible moment.
Bell County tomorrow.
Yeah, um . . . are you making the trip?
Dad wants to see y'all on the road again.
I pumped my fist in the air and tried not to dance around.
Do you want to go?
I think so.
Oh, man. That sounds . . . great.
It'll be a late night, but I'll bring my pillow.
Sure. We'll try to not let it go into overtime, I said, trying to sound confident.
They're fifth in the state, she added, like it was a nail in our coffin.
Roger that. Do you think we can win?
I think y'all have already surprised folks.
But what do YOU think?
I'll see you tomorrow.

PLAYLIST

After listening to Melophobia on repeat for
two hours nonstop
I took the ear buds   out.

Mike chewed bubble gum and gave Ozzie   wet willies.

The bus driver, Mr. Haven, looked with eagle eyes at each of   us.

The road was bumpy in places, and I could smell manure from the barns
we passed.

Shew, Cade complained, raising up his window and clicking it   into
place.

Coach was doing a crossword puzzle on his   lap.

I thought of the gym, the packed bleachers, a   girl.

The miles wheeled by and I imagined spin moves around not one but two
defenders.

I thought of sounds like *crash, swish, and*   ROAR.

DUNK YOU, VERY MUCH

Mike grabbed the tip, dished to me, and immediately sliced to the rim.
I heaved a pass from the hip and placed it right in his upward FLIGHT.

I want to be like Mike! I shouted over the silenced crowd.

He high-fived me, and we hustled back
on defense.

Coach called for a half-court press, and
we hiked up our ball shorts and
Willie smacked the floor with both hands
like the punk he was.

We got a five-second call against Bell County's best guard.
The ball was ours again.

I scanned the crowd only in the final seconds of our WIN.
She was there, beside her dad, clapping.
She held a popcorn carton, spilling it as she clapped.

The Seton jersey
felt nice against my sweaty skin.

Mike had notched a forty-point game, and one of the assistants
told me I had eighteen assists and a double-double, with
fourteen points.

I nodded like I was listening, but I only saw the brunette with her
popcorn.

BANK SHOT (THE BANK IS OPEN)

Our first tournament of the new year,
and I guarded the PG from another
small school.

I felt *so* confident as the clock clicked
down:

Five seconds—We had a timeout and Coach didn't signal a T with his hand.
Four seconds —*I got you, player. #42 ain't going to let you drive the lane.*
Three seconds—PG crossed me over, and I almost fell for it. Still no T from Coach.
Two seconds—We're up two. ANYTHING inside the three is a trip to overtime.
Not on my watch.
One second—*We're in the 1-and-1 bonus. I can foul him before . . .*

Forget this.

He jumped up for a long three. I rose with him, and we were eye level. He let go of the rock, and I actually felt my fingertips strike leather as it went up UP UP!

The ball traveled in a nice rainbow arc, and the gym went silent. The ball cascaded against the glass and banked into the hoop. The buzzer BUZZED like a swarm of summer crickets.

We lost.

I hung my head, pulled my jersey up into my mouth.

It was a loooooong bus ride back to Seton.

10-3

The next practice was anything but   perfect.
We ran zombie-like through the drills.   It felt like boot camp.
FYI: That's where my brother was   Quantico.
He trained to fight in a war.
I thought of Virginia, and it felt like the   end of the earth.
Then, I thought of Isis, and for some reason,   she made me think of ISIS.
The Taliban were out there somewhere, and my brother was RUNNING at them.
I trusted Skylar to protect himself; that's what he'd always done   for me.
He stood up to *my* bullies,   before he left.
Now, I thought of bullies with machine guns, and I prayed for him.
I ran up and down the cold, dusty court, and I   prayed.
I prayed he wouldn't be one of the casualties they talked about on   CNN.

Skylar, take care of yourself.
Bullies don't stop   *in REAL life.*

WATER BREAK

We called Ozzie the team camel,
because he drank all the water in the fountain.
We only had a few seconds between breaks in practice,
but he didn't mind.

He *slurp slurp SLURPED* the water down into his never full stomach.
And we waited.
For him to rise up and go,
AHHH, That's cold!

And when he did, we'd push him aside, eager
for that slightly less cold taste.

You drank all the cold water! Willie shouted, smacking Ozzie on the head.

The water warmed and warmed
as we waited in line.
By the time I got there, the water was
no longer cool.
Lukewarm.
I sipped for a few seconds, and then,
I heard Coach's whistle, commanding us
back to the hardwood.

BLOCK PARTY

Mike had such long arms he blocked
EVERYTHING
we heaved up to the basket in practice.

We tried pump fakes
and fadeaways
and hook shots
even,
but he was inescapable.

We couldn't shake those spider legs,
those tentacle arms.
They suctioned onto every ball we
launched.

And he batted it down. He palmed it mid-air,
and I saw him smile ever-so-slightly.
He knew, before the ball left our hands, that
he had it.

Coach didn't have to tell him where to stand,
how to position himself.

He had a *high basketball IQ*, Coach said.
It's just something he knows how to do.
The ball is magnetized to his palm.

When a shot came inside, we knew
Mike had it.

It was TORTURE. We all became
sharp-shooters from deep. We NEVER took it
inside.

But in actual games, we smiled, when opponents
drove the lane.
We knew the spider was waiting for anything round to
try and take a shot at its web.

BIG CITY

The Lexington school came down to Seton
and we warmed-up like we always did.
I lined our JV squad up, and Cade Rainey drove in
for our first layup.
I followed him, one dribble, two dribbles, up and
IN.
I caught the ball through the net, and my mind
ZOOMED to Mike.
Was he somewhere in the stands?
Why wasn't he here?
Of all games, this one was a chance to beat some
big city cats.
I knew he wouldn't miss it for the world.
These guys were next-door neighbors to
UK.
It was his chance to say, *I'll show them fellas how MJ*
did it.

For me, it was a chance to prove myself against future
college talent. Many of those Lexington guys would
play D-1.
I looked for scouts, and I knew several notepads were there
just for Mike.

But he was nowhere to be found.
I knew his home life
wasn't perfect.
His mom had passed.
His dad was disabled.
Still, Mike wasn't there, and
he *never* missed a game.

The tip went off, and the beat-down began.

I netted a few from deep, and Cade
matched me with a few shots
from the elbow.
But Mike wasn't there, and we lost the lead.
The notepads went away, and the crowd
lost interest.
We stumbled and fell, and I couldn't do anything
without him.

Mike, where are you?

TECHNICAL

The next day at school
Mike came in late.

Counselor Swann walked him to English,
and our teacher stopped talking.

Take a seat, Mike, he said.
Then, he droned on about *The Giver*.

He said words like *utopia* and *slavery*,
and I saw a swirl of robots and sad people.
I thought of home, and Mom, and I tried to think happy thoughts.

Then, I saw Mike staring at his worn copy of the book,
and I knew something was definitely UP.

At lunch, he told me his dad had a *spell*.

What's wrong with him?

He fell again, and he wouldn't get up.

Ohhhh, man.

Yeah. I found him like that and dialed 9-1-1.

They say he was all right?

They say he shouldn't be alone.

Are you . . .

They're bringing in an aide.

To help him?

Yeah. They're gonna be there to make sure he's okay.

I didn't say anything else.
Mike picked up his rectangle of pizza and stared at it.
I felt like *The Giver* was coming to life, and it felt cold.

The lunchroom watched as we sat in silence.

TONIC-CLONIC SEIZURES

I rolled the words around in my head.
Mike wasn't at practice either.
Coach blew the whistle with crazy force.

Mike will be back, he said afterwards.

Tonic-Clonic
Tonic-Clonic
Tonic-Clonic

They're Grand Mal seizures, Mom told me at home.
*You remember the one that Grandma had
that time.*

I thought of Grandma's house, the time she
rolled around on the floor.

Will it happen again?

We pray it doesn't, she said. *Just pray it won't.*

So, I went to bed that night and prayed.
I clasped my hands together and prayed for
Mike's dad.

I heard the ring-ring-ring on my cell phone.
It was Isis, and she said, *I'm thinking of you.*

*I was just thinking of Mike.
Me, too.
Couldn't sleep.
Me, either.
Think his dad will be okay?*

I think he's Mike's dad, and you know what that means?

I smiled at the glowing screen and listened to her voice.
Yeah, I knew what that meant. He was a tough, tough fighter.

The seconds on the call climbed, and I thought of the seconds in the game going down to the buzzer.

POST UP (BOX OUT)

Cade Rainey shifted to center.

The absence in the paint was strong.
Without Mike, practice was
a GAPING hole.

We drove and finger-rolled it over the top of
Rainey's head.

He couldn't stop us. He was about my height.
The assistants gave him pointers, but it didn't
help.

Box out for the rebound! Coach hollered at
Cade.

We scored inside at will, and practice was
a JOKE.

It was odd not seeing Mike in the locker room.
It felt like a ghost was there, and I was
spooked.

CHOCOLATE MILK

Isis loved chocolate milk. So, I gave her mine
in the caf.

The milk carton's sweat ran
down its side.

Don't you need strong bones?

I smiled at her. My first in a while.

Mike sat across from us and

stroked his mustache.

You need to eat, man, I said.

He shrugged his shoulders and stared at the tray.

We play Pulaski soon, and you need to FLEX.

He paused mid-stroke and pushed his tray away.
Isis cleared her throat and slowly opened the paper, milk carton.

Pulaski, man. Those guys are hulks! I said.

Isis sipped at the milk and sipped.
I poked around at my spaghetti with a fork.
Mike bit his lip and didn't say anything.

We need you back, man. Those guys won't stand a chance against YOU.

Basketball is a team sport, Bobcat, Isis said.

I know that, Isis, but I'm just trying to get our center back.

Mike got up to empty his untouched tray. He tossed
it all away and went to the exit.

GAME NIGHT AGAIN

The Pulaski squad was lit. They shot the lights out.
It was hard to keep up with their threes,
and Coach kept yelling for us to make OUR shots.

I knocked one down from the corner, and Willie hit a surprise three himself.

I always loved unexpected daggers.

Ozzie came off the bench and knocked down a three-point play.

I'm 'and-one' all day, he bragged.

Don't get cocky.

Mike stood under the basket (on both ends of the court) and went through the motions.

We were tied up with a minute to play.

Isis cheered from the stands, and I saw her whisper something into her dad's ear.
The popcorn was passed back and forth between them.

Eyes on the game, Bobcat, Coach barked.

I looked and saw Mike with one defender on him.
I gave my head nod, and he didn't acknowledge.
I did the head nod again, and Mike shook his head *NO*.

I drove down the lane and let a floater fly his way.

Surprisingly he rose up, caught it midair, and

LAYED IT IN.

The crowd, expecting the dunk, hushed.
Even a few *BOOS* erupted.
I didn't say anything. Mike was fouled on the play.
With time running out, he rattled in a free throw
from the charity stripe.

It was a road win, even if our center was way off.

VISIT

Dad was away on work most of the year but not today.
He drove a semi-truck, and he parked it in our front yard.
The goal was open, because he never parked under it.

It was an unspoken rule.

Mike came over, Mom begged him to.
We played a little one-on-one, and Dad
asked if he could play.

Before supper, we worked up a sweat, and the metal
chains on the net went SWISH, SPLASH, SWISH.
Dad smacked Mike on the back and told him he was
unstoppable.

We had strawberry jam, from berries Mom grew in our garden.
We slathered them onto homemade biscuits, and I looked
at Mike.

I heard *MMM* sounds again and again, as he licked his fingers.
I did, too.

Nothing was as good as *that* dessert.

Dad fired the semi to life and took Mike home.
The sun was down, and I felt happy for the first time that week.

RALLY HATS

Coach wanted us to full-court press
the heck out of everyone else we played that season.

We practiced inbounds plays until we were
BLUE in the face.

We did it for Mike as much as anyone.

If we could keep the opponent from inbounding the ball,
that meant less work on the other end of the court.

It meant turnovers
like apple
and cherry
and that seasonal one they had at Smitty's restaurant—
PUMPKIN.

I loved those things.
I thought of them year-round.
I joined Willie in smacking the court,
no longer feeling like he was a punk for doing it.

It *was* WAR.
And I thought of my brother, Skylar, shooting
a weapon to survive.

I didn't even like shooting at deer.
I didn't want to harm anything, unless
it had a basketball in its hands.

Coach blew the whistle, and I said,
Mike don't do anything. We got this!

And we kept the JV second-string from bringing
the ball across mid-court ONCE.

It was battle, and I was some kind of
captain.

I took it personal, and I wanted the white, surrender flag
waved in defeat.

FREE WEIGHTS

Cade cranked the tunes UP
on the stereo.

It was MAX-OUT day.

We needed all the motivation we could get.

We started with the heavy weights.

Coach ROARED in our ears.

Was he a lion?

Were we his pride?

The Seton JV team grunted and roared back, trying to push the bar back to its home.

We kept out of Varsity squad's way.

Bench press was the ultimate challenge.

We put wagon wheels, forty-five pounds apiece, on the bar and LIFTOFF.

We worked down to five pounders and were huffing and puffing as Coach told us the count.

On the final, five reps, it was just us versus THE BAR.

And even though it only weighed like fifteen pounds, it felt like GAZILLIONS!

Mike did it all without so much as a loud breath.

Was my friend in there? Had a robot replaced him?

I turned red in the face, and I felt sweat running down my spine. It clung to my shirt, and I felt like the bench was glued to my back.

Three, two, one . . . and Coach just held his hand under the bar, and I willed it back into its cradle.

That's what I'm talking about, Bobcat! That's team spirit! he beamed.

QUINTUPLE-DOUBLE

I got Mike to talking about the impossible
quintuple-double.

Five double-digit stats for a player, like:
points
rebounds
assists
steals
and blocks.

(It was a trick I'd used more than once.)

No one had ever done it
in the modern era.
It was a dagger to his ego, and Mike stopped
unlacing his shoes after practice.

I tossed my kicks into the locker. They smelled
TERRIBLE.

I think you could do it.

I KNOW I could.

I was so glad I had him talking, smiling even,
that I forgot to say more.

He picked up his gym bag, and I saw the Converse
logo on the side.

I thought you were all Nike.

Times change.

MJ shoes ain't gonna like this.

He smiled again, said, *I don't care what MJ rides think.*

Are you gonna start wearing Chucks on the court?

Yeah. I'm gonna wear slouchy socks, too. Big old floppy things you can't MISS. When I block everybody. I might even block you.

I was stoked to see him joking.
I wondered if his home life was better.

I didn't ask, because he elbowed me in the ribs and said, Quintuple-doubles, man. I don't think they're as rare as unicorns. You can see them. You're gonna see one
real soon. I promise.

RUN-AND-GUN

Mike knew how much I always wanted to do
the run-and-gun offense.

Coach shook his head every time
I forgot to finish the play.

I didn't want to run an elevator screen and
shift defenders one way or another.
I just wanted to SCORE.

Mike knew this.
He knew me better than anyone.

We brought the ball up all night long
on a weaker, slower district rival.

The game wasn't even close.
I had one mission—let the shots fall.

Mike grabbed boards and chucked them
out to me and Cade.

We were knocking down jump shots.

Before I knew what the score even was,
an assistant told me I had twenty points.

More than that, Mike had a dozen rebounds.
He ATTACKED the backboard
like an angry German Shepherd that once chased us
around our park's baseball diamond.

Mike told me, *That's ten assists, Bobcat.*

He was straight money.
He blocked everything brought to him on D.
He was swatting peoples' shots like a flyswatter.

BZZZ CLAP CLAP CLAP

That's twelve blocks, bruh.

Coach was watching,
not even calling T to give us a breather.
We weren't winded, because Mike
was playing like a maniac.

He stole basketballs on each possession.
The undersized rival,
matching up with him in the post,
couldn't control the ball.

He put on a clinic.

If steals could've been counted against us,
he would've taken the ball
FROM us.
With the clock winding down,
he quit defending players in the post.
He wasn't under the goal
but out at the three guarding
MY GUY.

I stood there dumbstruck,
and Mike guided the shooter over to me,
and he said, *Bobcat. Double team!*

I snapped out of my trance-like state,
and I put my hands on the ball
to take it away.
No you don't, Mike roared. *It's mine.*

The clock echoed around the Seton gym,
and he did it.
Mike had stolen his tenth ball,
and the stat was no longer a unicorn.
It was there on the spreadsheet.
The statistician stood
at the scorer's table and applauded.

The entire gym was aware
of what he'd done.

The benchwarmers ran to him.
He dribbled the ball at mid-court,
and Coach shook hands with our deflated rival.

FOUR HIGH

After Mike's clinic,
we moved to a four high play.

We wanted to give the seven-footer the ENTIRE paint.

Coach said, *Just stay out of his way. He'll take care of the rest.*

Iso, Iso, the opposing coach shouted at the top of his lungs. *COLLAPSE!*

And the other team all raced to the paint to SWARM Mike like an angry nest of
HORNETS.

They BUZZED and YELLED at him to try and distract him, but he was deaf to the
sound.

Mike pivoted between the dogpile,
and he pump-faked a defender.
Then, he did it to a second guy.
He put the ball on the hardwood once
and caught it.
He let gravity do the trick and
he rose like the Statue of Liberty and
he brought the ball back with both hands
behind his head and
THUNDERED home a dunk,
raising his knees up like Shaq and
clapping the backboard with one hand
on the way back to earth.

The other coach called *TIMEOUT,* and
we smacked Mike on the back.

We hustled to the bench where
the Powerade never tasted so sweet.

SCOUTS

The dunk was on SportsCenter!

Mike actually signed autographs
the next day at school.

Seton's Varsity coach, Coach Turpin, wanted to know if he'd like to move up and forget JV.

You have waaaaay more talent than any player I've ever seen at Seton.

Mike stroked his mustache and looked around Coach Turpin's office.
FYI: I lingered at the door and listened.
I wanted Mike to stay with us; we were mid-season.
But I wanted him to do what was right for #23, too.

I tried to not be jealous, but the words were there
HOVERING around the stale, trophy-lined room.

What would he say?
Who would turn down THAT offer, as a eighth grader?

I cleared my throat and hoped Coach Turpin hadn't heard me. It wouldn't be a good way to begin my relationship with him—an EAVESDROPPER. But Mike just rubbed the palms of his long fingers on his blue jeans like he always did. He stood to leave and patted the back of the faux leather chair.

Think about it, son. You could be putting up these stats against REAL opponents. Not JV kids.

Mike laughed and saw me creeping in the hallway.

I have a squad, and we're tight already. I'll get there, Coach. I want to finish THIS season though.

You're risking it all, Mike. Staying down there. Think about your future. The scouts already are, son.

I am, and I'm not risking a thing.

PICK AND ROLL

The Seton JV squad gelled better than ever after Mike's sit-down with Coach Turpin.
Mike lunged after every loose ball.
I chased down opponents and forced turnovers.
The ball was ours and we HAD TO HAVE IT.

Coach was afraid to call timeout, even when we were up thirty one night.
He didn't want momentum to be lost.
Mike set high screens and we
PICK and ROLLED like an
ocean wave.

Defenders didn't know what hit them.
We shared the ball, and I felt like I was
walking on water.

Hey, Bobcat, Cade said at halftime. *Let's switch sides . . . confuse them.*

And we did. We ran half-court offenses with Willie bringing the ball up, and Cade ran from the left side under the hoop and I ran from the right, and we high-fived midway and ended up on opposite wings.

The cheerleaders went wild, chanting:

S-E-T-O-N
L-I-O-N-S
that's who we are
THAT'S WHO WE ARE

The pep band played the school song, and everything was money.

We were even graced with the Varsity squad's presence, and more than a few shouted at Mike, *Get with the picture.* WE WANT YOU, MULANEY!

Mike focused on blocking his opponent, creating turnovers, and then doing what he did best— rattling the rim with as much force as all one-hundred-thirty pounds could.

DECISIONS

Isis asked me if I thought Mike would join Varsity squad.
I shrugged and stood still as a cactus.

You know he could get hurt playing JV. That'd be tragic, Levi.

She called me by my name, and it jarred me.

He IS on ESPN, she added. *Shouldn't he be more careful?*

I let the SportsCenter reel roll through my brain. It was a DREAM for anyone.

He's not going to get hurt, Isis. What makes you say that?

She wedged her arm into my ribcage and walked me to fifth period.

I smelled Sweet Pea, her scent.
It smelled like a big field of flowers.

Where'd you get that perfume?

Don't change the subject.

I love it.

She smiled and hugged me.

I thought of Mike rolling his ankle and instantly tried to push the image away.

He was Shaq in the flesh; the best player we'd ever had at Seton, and I couldn't imagine him not being there. I didn't want to.

DEFENSIVE SHIFT

We moved to Zone D   with three out and two in.
Coach said it would help us guard   *outside* shots.
Mike could collapse on those inside and   clean up the scraps.
It helped quite a bit and not one shooter   tried to go inside.
Those shooters on the wing were afraid of   the middle.
And, we did our best to contest every three   they sent up.
The scores were smaller, and we'd found   a new way to win.

LUNCH

At lunch, an alien form of beef was on the menu. I forked it over and looked on both sides. It was brown and slimy with a few fake grill marks down the middle.

It's Salisbury steak, Mike said with familiarity. *You too good for THAT, bruh?*

I shook my head and looked at the gravy-like gel it floated in.
(I was happy he was talking.)

Isis scooted her tray back and put her head on my shoulder.

It's not really meat, she said. *I might go vegan. I've been thinking about it.*

Good luck with that.

I pushed down on it with the backside of my fork, and the gel slowly rose to the top of the patty.

It got me thinking about the *B-E-E-F* technique Coach yelled about in practice.

It went Balance-Eyes-Elbow-Follow Through—a shooter's rule, and I committed it to memory. The meat in front of me was a poor reminder, but I said the words over and over to myself:

Balance-Eyes-Elbow-Follow Through Balance-Eyes-Elbow-Follow Through
Balance-Eyes-Elbow-Follow Through Balance-Eyes-Elbow-Follow Through
Balance-Eyes-Elbow-Follow Through Balance-Eyes-Elbow-Follow Through
Balance-Eyes-Elbow-Follow Through . . .

just like Salisbury steak.

HEALTHY

Isis *did* stop eating meat   ALL of it.
She started doing these crazy   diets, too.
I didn't like anything with the word *DIE*   in it.
She carried crackers from the caf, and she ate from her purse.
There were packets of honey she smuggled and squeezed   onto them.
It went on for a few weeks, and she started to look really   pale.

Hey, is your girl all right, Bobcat?

I don't know, I said. (Because I didn't.)

She even stopped taking my FREE chocolate milks I gave her.

She lost a lot of weight, and her dad picked her up from school one day.

I hoped she was okay.

BUMP

We played a game called Bump at my house.
The game was fairly simple:

The first shooter took a shot from the three, and if he/she made it,
the next person in line shot.
If the first person missed, the next shooter lined up a dagger and shot,
trying to 'bump' that person out.
The goal was to be the last person *alive*.

After that, we just goofed around.

Isis was a good sport, but her color was still way off.
She looked pale pale PALE.

She became so tired, she wasn't even able to get her layups to fall.

Mike looked at me, and I didn't know what to do.

It wasn't too much fun, as Isis sat down and watched from the sidelines.

Mom came out and said dinner was almost ready.

Are you eating, Isis? I made plenty of fried chicken for everyone.

Isis grabbed her stomach and said she couldn't stay. She had to get home.

I offered to go with her, but she shook her head, picked up her bike, and slowly rode
away.

PHYSICAL

Isis' dad took her to the doctor, the only doctor in Seton, Dr. Scruggs.
He said she had an *eating disorder.*

I saw the honey packets and crackers (in my mind) the minute Isis' dad repeated it—
eating disorder.

The words made me hate Salisbury steak, the caf.
She said she was fine.
I went to her house that night to make sure.
She was propped up on some pillows and was watching
Gilmore Girls on Netflix.

I never understood that show.

It's all about the mom and daughter.

I know. I just don't see why they talk so fast.

Their brains work on OVERLOAD.

And that's funny?

It's just who they are.

Oh.

Isis rearranged the pillows behind her back, and her dad brought some OJ and dinner.

Are you having to take anything?

Levi, I'm getting my strength back. I'm not dying or anything.

I nodded like I understood, but I just wanted to see the color return to her cheeks.
FYI: she was way TOO thin.

Let's let her eat this grilled cheese, her dad said.

I walked out with him and he told me to stop by anytime.

When will she be back at Seton, Mr. Dupree?

Soon. Very soon.

HEROES

MJ missed over 9,000 shots in his career, and still,
#23 was a hero to us.
Mike wanted to be a Tar Heel someday because of him.
MJ lived in the gym.
Plus, he played baseball and golf.
I saw a magazine of him once smoking a cigar.
I wondered what it tasted like.
Dad wasn't home one weekend, and I offered one of his to Mike, and I took one, too.
We cut the ends, as I'd seen Dad do countless times.
I lit the end for Mike, and then I did the same for mine.
We puffed on them and went *UGGGGHHH*
We coughed for hours.
Mom came out on the porch and smelled it, before she saw us.
She got the broom and chased us off into the woods.
We spit and spit and thought we were losing our lungs.
It was the last time we did EVERYTHING MJ did.

BASKETBALL/LOVE

Willie asked me what I loved more:

Basketball or . . .
Isis.

Seriously?

Yes, dummy. The 5' 6" blonde you're always dialing on your cell, or, hoops?

I let the question hang there like a kite.
He was such a punk. All the TIME.
I didn't even want to give him the satisfaction of an answer.
I thought about her coming to that first game.
The denim jacket and popcorn were locked in my mind.

I guess I'd have to say—give me that, as I smacked the ball out of his hand.

He chased me down the court, and I launched a shot from half-court.
It banked in, and he laughed.

So, that's your answer?

That's one answer.

NO PAIN NO GAIN

I mangled my finger doing a finger roll near the rim.
It was stupid really.
It wasn't even practice. Just a pickup game during
free period at Seton.

Coach was LIVID.

He grabbed my hand right when it happened.
I looked down and saw the damage.
It wasn't a break either.
It was a *dis-location*.
My middle finger on my shooting hand, turned at a sic angle.

The guy who did it, turned away and said, *I'm sorry, Bobcat.*

I felt the pop and almost passed out just looking at it. The finger turned BLUE immediately.

Put it back, I told Coach.

He said, *Look the other way*, and tugged on the middle digit.

It wouldn't budge, and so we went to the nurse.
She turned PINK and said go to Seton Hospital.
We did, and the wait was TWO HOURS.

When the doctor finally saw us, he snapped his fingers together and said, *Hold on.*

He came back with a syringe and numbed my lop-sided finger. Then, he said, *This will still hurt*, and tugged on it until it went *POP!* again.

I felt sweaty all over, and he told Coach to give me time to heal.

But we played a district game the next day, and I had one of the assistant managers wrap it in good tape.

I couldn't stop playing all because of a finger.

SUPERVISION

Mike watched his dad pick up the coffee mug and sip a slooooooow sip.

Let me make you a fresh cup, Pops.

Mike's dad waved him away.
This is fine. Ahhh! Nothing like a cup of coffee.

No cream, no sugar, Mike joined in.

The two laughed in unison.
I watched and looked at Mr. Mulaney for any signs, shakes.
He held the cup steadier than a gunslinger.
I wished my middle finger felt that good.
I looked down and saw it purpley-blue inside the wrap.

That hand is gonna need some time to heal.

I looked at this man who'd just shook a life-or-death blow and smiled.

No time. We play on Friday. Ain't that right, Mike?

Mike gazed at his dad.

Mike. Yo, Mike. Earth to the seven-footer. We gotta play, don't we?

Well, I'd let that heal. The court'll be there, whenever you're back to good, Mr. Mulaney said, smiling over his mug.

Friday is district. We gotta bring it, I said, trying to sound tough.

Mike looked away from his dad and play swatted at my hand.

I jerked away in time. It was a new game we'd started. 'Try and hit Bobcat's Hand.' If I dodged it, my reflexes were game ready. So far, I'd received a smack on the first attempt from Mike's GARGANTUAN paws and learned from nearly passing out from the pain—once was
ENOUGH.

I see those reflexes, Mr. Mulaney chimed in. *But can you still shoot the rock?*

I stood from the musty sofa and mimicked my B-E-E-F skill, holding the follow through for five seconds.

Good form. Now, only game time will tell if all this holds any weight. If I feel up to it, I'll be there courtside, too.

I was thrilled to hear it—after his Tonic-Clonic episode.
Mike jumped up from the cushions, too, and gave his old man a big squeeze. I'd never seen Mike so happy. His mustache was buried in the folds of Mr. Mulaney's flannel shirt.

PROMISES

Mr. Mulvaney was true to his word and sat front row for Friday's game.
I noticed just a few people sitting in his vicinity, and I thought of stupid prejudices.
It made my vision blurry and my hand THROBBED!

I wanted to give him a hug and say, *Mr. Mulaney, I want to be strong like you.*

Mike played strong enough for everyone on the Seton squad that night.
His man couldn't guard him, and they started double-teaming him.
When we went to the huddle during timeouts, he sipped his Powerade and stared over at his dad.

The coast is CLEAR, he said.

So, is the wing, I said. *Skip one out to me. They're triple-teaming you now.*

He dribbled once in the post and dished the rock to me. I caught it in rhythm and let the B-E-E-F FLY!
Up Up UP to the rim and I watched it CLACK off the back iron. I put my arm down and hustled back on defense.

Mr. Mulaney cheered, and he yelled, *Keep shooting, Bobcat!*

I missed and missed and still he cheered. Mom did, too. Isis was beside her.
(BUT I was MISSING everying!)
It didn't matter. We were up twenty and Mike was on the verge of a triple-double that night.

BALL DON'T LIE

I was 2-12 from the field. Ball don't lie, Mike.

Nope. It sure don't. We won by twenty-two. Even if you were SALISBURY STEAK, Bobcat!

I let the new joke settle in and accidentally hit my finger against the locker.

YYYYOWWW! I roared at the metal door, cupping my shooting hand.

That locker don't hit back, man.

I nodded, tears forming in the corners of my eyes.

It didn't matter, bruh. The TEAM won. We're moving on. We can say NEXT!

Why was everyone cheering, even when I missed?

We gelled, man. We were unstoppable, even with your brick house.

I laughed through the tears and felt the finger *thump thumping* like a heartbeat.

That tape threw your shot WAY off, Mike added. *You'll get used to those fingers being taped together. Don't worry.*

I looked down and hated seeing it wrapped like an egg roll. The middle finger was dragging me down.

Hey . . . We won.

DOUBLE DRIBBLE

When we weren't alley-ooping on NBA Street, Mike went even more old school and
showed me his dad's retro NES system.
He had a game called Double Dribble, and
you had to blow on the cartridge to make it play.
The game had some WONKY graphics, and
it froze up almost ten times in a row, but
the cut scenes when a player dunked were KILLER.

Mike said, *Watch this*, and
he drove one of his Lakers players to the basket.
The game paused and
a cut scene showed a dude dunking in slow motion.
It was simple, but
so tight!

My team was the Celtics and
Larry Bird was shooting from everywhere.
I laughed when he hit a shot from half-court.

Mike dunked and dunked, and
we high-fived each other every time one of his Lakers went up over a Celtic and
slammed the ball home.

Isis didn't want to play, but
she offered hilarious play-by-play as the game went on.

She said things like, *Why are their shorts sooooo short?*
And, *Could a player really shoot from that spot?*
And my favorite, *What's with the slow-mo stuff?*

We cracked up every time, and

she lost interest and started asking Mr. Mulaney stuff about the house like,

How long have y'all lived here?
Do you have any coffee left?
Are THOSE baby pictures of Mike?

We paused on the last one, but
even Mike couldn't pull himself away from Double Dribble.

Mr. Mulaney showed her pictures, saying,

This here's a picture of Mike's mom. She was a GREAT woman.

Isis didn't ask what'd happened to her.

This is little Mike getting his first bath.
We couldn't get him out of the tub.
He loved that warm, sudsy water so much.
Oh, and this is when he caught his first fish.

I elbowed Mike, holding the controller, trying
to punch buttons with my injured paw.

Thought you didn't like to fish?

I'd rather EAT fish, he said, grinning, eyes locked on the next cut scene.

You think anyone else at Seton ever played Double Dribble?

Mike hit the pause button, his hands covering the entire controller.
He stroked the mustache and said, *I bet no one even knows it EXISTS.*

THIS IS WAR

I tried to imagine all of the skills I'd need to use to beat Pulaski again.
They were the biggest squad in our district.
They had five dudes all shorter than Mike, but they were muscled up, Terminator guys.
My brain fired on all cylinders before the game.
I thought of Coach's barks, his babblings from a year's worth of practices.

It rattled around in my brain like one big mess:

Ball-You-Man. Ball-YOU-Man, Bobcat!
Don't give up a foul. Don't send them to the line. Unless, you have a foul to GIVE.
We don't want to rely on any Buzzer Beaters!
Don't let them get past you. Don't let them get in the BONUS. Stop your dribble drive, ON A DIME.
Pull up and shoot the J, or, kick it to a teammate.
COLLAPSE their D.
If you're at the top of the key, weigh all your options, boys!
If you pull the trigger, follow your shot. CRASH THE BOARDS.
If they drive on you, don't give an inch. Ride their hip.
Get your feet planted, if you're in front of them, and flop.
Be like Tom Hanks and ACT. Take the dadblamed CHARGE! There are NO tomorrows.
It's just this one game.
No Pain. No GAIN.
You got me?
Everyone is oh and oh. Zero Wins. Zero Losses.
I don't want to see any weak floaters or finger rolls.
You take the rock to the basket with AUTHORITY.
You help your teammates. You fast break like your life depends on it. 'Cuz it does!
You give-and-go and don't let up until the whistle blows.
From tip to that final drive, you go HARD.

If the ball is loose, so are you!
If you get trapped, you think before you call a timeout. We need all of them.
I call the T. I'll substitute you when you're winded.
If you lose your man, you better . . . well, you better NOT! I want help side D all night.
This is Pulaski. They will make you pay.
Mike, don't goaltend. If the shot goes up, it goes up. If it goes in, well, it's in.
But, don't pluck anything around the circle.
Keep your spacing until they DRIVE. And these rhinos will drive with their heads down.
They'll CRASH through you, or, try to. But if your feet are set, the whistle will blow.
If it doesn't, well . . . let me handle that part.
Steal anything they put in your path. Look to INTERCEPT their mid-court passes.
They will try to make it through the press.
But you're Seton Lions, aren't you? Well?
Who ARE YOU?!

Seton Lions! we roared back at him from the bench, warmup pants being popped off.
We threw our shooting shirts to the team manager.
The assistant coach helped him collect the discarded clothes.

And one more thing fellas . . .
We have the best frontcourt in all of Kentucky. I mean that.
Coach Turpin wanted to pluck Mike here away. Take that as your vote of confidence.
I have faith in all of you.
Mike, he's a heckuva playmaker. Let him do the dirty work inside.
Bobcat, the tip is OURS.
Mike will get it.
It's your job to keep the plays moving.
How's your hand by the way?

I went from one hundred to two miles-per-hour, when he asked it. Every bit of school spirit PAUSED.

All of the guys looked from me to the Pulaski squad stretching, shooting layups.

Not wanting to let anyone in the gym down, especially Coach, I shook the taped fingers back and forth like a chicken testing its wings.

Let's do this, I said.

XS AND OS

Cade Rainey took a lot of the weight off my shoulders—
tipping in missed shots and scrambling for loose balls.
He was part seal, SLIDING on his belly across the court.

Look at that boy, GO! Coach was shouting, getting the other assistant coaches to join in.

Cade was all over the place. He saw me protecting my hand on rebounds, and Mike was triple-teamed by the wider, beefier Pulaski guys.
It was a spectacle. We were watching Cade work. He was HUSTLING like someone late for their flight.
Cade drew fouls from two of Pulaski's best shooters and put them in foul trouble early. They sat on the bench most of the second quarter.
He took advantage and caught assists from Mike and Willie over and over again. It was a constant shifting of the D—inside to Mike, outside to Willie, and back to the blonde-haired lightning bolt, Cade.
Despite all of his hustle, the game was still close. One Pulaski guard, not hurt by fouls stood on the wing and made a couple of buckets over Willie.
I switched with him on D.

I had him, Willie whined.

Sure you DID.

I tried to take the Pulaski kid's ball, but my injured finger struck his hand, and I bent over in pain.

T, Ref, T.

Coach led me to the sideline, and my eyes blurred with tears.

I can handle it, Coach.

Not right now. We'll use you in the fourth.

And just like that we had our sixth man out there trying to defend a guy THREE TIMES his size.
The score was knotted up twenty-eight all.
The third quarter was back and forth. Mike squeezed in a few cleanup shots Cade missed.
We went four high and made the defense spread out on us.
Cade hit a few outside jumpers and
a second defender was put on him.
I checked in and took my spot on the wing.
(FYI: The fourth quarter was ROUGH.)
There were a couple of flagrant fouls delivered by two guys collapsing on Mike.
He let out a grunt, when an ELBOW went to his sternum.
I hustled over and helped him up with my GOOD hand.

This is IT.

I know that #23, you good?

Mike gripped his ribcage and nodded like Apollo Creed.

Call the FOUL, ZEBRA, or, I'll make this your last game.

Don't step out of the box, or, I'll give you a technical, Coach.

The final sixty seconds clicked down.
Cade still had two guards favoring him.
I needed to step up NOW.
I called for Willie to give me the ball.

But the play, Bobcat.

Tell Coach I'll apologize later.

He gave me the ball reluctantly, and I dribbled over to the edge of the sideline. I crossed over one defender and switched back to my good hand. Another came at me, and I gave him the same treatment.
OUCH my hand.
DRIBBLE DRIBBLE DRIBBLE
Fifteen seconds.
I didn't want a five-second call. I reversed the ball over to Ozzie. He caught it, and I saw
FEAR in his eyes.
Just as quickly, I called for it back. He heaved it like a WOBBLY football.
Eight seconds.
The crowd was IRATE. There was so much maroon color in the crowd, I looked down at the ball and said, THIS IS IT.
Four seconds. I spin-moved around one beast, and I met his friend. I kept the ball in my strong hand.
Two seconds. I went up for a layup and felt a linebacker wrap me up in a tackle. The ball fell out of my shooting hand and landed nowhere near the rim.
The buzzer went off, and the guy who hit me got up and cheered.

TAKE THAT!

The ref blew his whistle and the crowd stopped booing.

TWO SHOTS! he shouted. *He's going to the LINE!*

The Pulaski player put his hands to his lips, bit his fingertips.
Everyone lined up around the foul line.

Coach said, *One to tie, Bobcat. One to tie.*

I dribbled 1-2-3 and spun the ball in front of me. I caught it and lined up the first shot.
I used my wobbly legs to give as much lift to the shot as I could.
It went up, hit the back rim, rattled on both sides and fell in.
Tied.

This one's nowhere close, the linebacker laughed. *Fifty dollars says it doesn't draw rim.*

I did my three dribble routine, caught it and paused. (I paused longer than I should have.)
I dribbled 1-2-3 and spun the ball in front of me again. This time, I pictured it hitting the back of the net, and I prayed it would.
I went up, the ball went out, and I was thinking *B-E-E-F, B-E-E-F, B-E-E-F* the whole time. The shot SWISHED through the net.

Coach got to me first, and he gripped me in a bear hug, and said, *Forget OVERTIME. Forget I said it. Forget IT!*

ZOO KEEPERS

Isis wanted to know why we called them that—
Zebras.

Besides the stripes they wear?

What more do you need? Mike asked.

I mean, it's not very clever.

Sure it is. When they're not blowing whistles, they look the part.

She looked over at me. I was munching on a pineapple tidbit.
They're just doing what they're supposed to do . . . calling the game.

That's just it. They're out there, and they're SUPPOSED to be fair. Sometimes they get it
right.

Against Pulaski, they called the foul, Mike agreed. *But there've been times when—*

When they don't blow the whistle.

They turn a blind eye, Mike added.

They get paid off, I said.

They get it wrong.

They're only human, Isis argued.

No. They're ZEBRAS, and they're calling stuff against Lions.

She laughed at us.

Mike high-fived me, and I mistakenly offered my bad hand.

The smack made me grab my wrist, and I felt like a total idiot.

We're Lions, and you know what Lions do? Mike said. *They EAT zebras. They EAT THEM!*

ISOLATION

Mike said that other game was
the first
his dad
had ever been to.

(I didn't remember him
ever
being at
another.)

He doesn't like the . . .
stares.

People don't stare, I lied.

He sat alone for practically that
whole game.

My dad doesn't want to cause
any trouble.

(I didn't know a kinder human.)

Didn't your dad and mine play together
back-in-the-day? I said, changing the subject.

Pops says they did.

Did yours play as good as you?

Bobcat, you know ain't NO ONE ever played like me
at Seton.

I laughed.

Seriously, you think anyone, even Pops, could take it away from me?

You need to gain about fifty pounds.

I eat waaaay more than you do.

I couldn't argue with that.
He was a string bean, and all he did was
EAT.
I heard him every
day at lunch:

Hey, you gonna eat that? Hey, don't throw that corn away! Hey, I'm a growing boy. Hey, didn't your momma raise you better?

Mike was our team's glue.

How could anyone hate the Mulaneys?

FAST BREAK

We lost the next game.   It wasn't even close.
Mike dunked until I   lost count.
His hands grew calluses   as the game wore on.
Coach had one play: 'dish it to Mike.'
None of us argued, because we were   WIPED.
The game before, against Pulaski, left all of us   scared to drive.
We flinched when we shot the ball   even WIDE open.
We looked like scared sheep being herded   into a tiny stall.
The zebras even looked braver than us.
Coach called timeouts and swapped us   in and out.
It was a revolving door of farm animals   until the BUZZER.
Our season was over, and that was our   fifth loss on the year.

SHOOTING RANGE

My hand healed up so slowwwwwwwwwwwwwly.
Coach Turpin got on Mike's case again, and said he'd do WHATEVER it took to see him play
VARSITY that same week.

That's a good problem to have, I admitted.

Zebras and poachers, man. What's a Lion to do?

I think you should play.

I'd said it before I really knew it.
Mike *was* wasting a great chance if he didn't dress out.
So, he dressed out.
The Seton Varsity jersey looked wicked on him.
He worked with an assistant coach to lift more weight, gain mass.
He even started their next game in region play.
His cheering section grew, with me joining Isis.
I watched his attack, his finesse at the rim. His footwork was cheddar.
He slashed and put the ball on the floor more.
Mike backed into defenders, raised his hand, and called—
Ball!

The Seton Varsity PG gave it to him.
Mike looked like a true center at work in the paint.
He skipped passes over the D and shared the ball with his *NEW* teammates.
Scouts were hungry in the crowd. Their pencils aimed at their
yellow legal pads.
They scribbled Mike's stats. They had a lot of
scribblescribblescribblescribblescribbles.
I saw them turn pages mid-quarter and lick their lips.
The Zebras let plays develop, and they even called touch fouls.
(I wished they'd done that in JV.)

Mike went to the line and looked for me in the crowd. His mouth moved to say something, but I couldn't make it out.

He's talking to you, Levi, Isis said.
She hugged my arm.

What's he saying?

I think he's saying, 'Watch this, Bobcat. Watch this.'

BEST FRIEND

I heard the front door bell go—
BING-BONG-BING.
I looked out the window and saw Mike and Isis
talking to each other.

Your folks home? Mike asked, as I opened the door.

Naw, it's just me.

Where's your ball?

Where it always is, I said, excited to dust it off, see if it still had air in it.

You haven't missed me too much have you?

I was beginning to wonder if you'd ever grace me with your PRESENCE!

Mike said, *Let's play around the world.*

What's that? Isis said.

Shooter's game. Bet I don't miss a shot, I said,
taking the ball away from Mike.

Them's fightin' words, bruh.

To the death.

Isis took the ball away from me and asked where the first shot went.

Through the hoop, babe.

Good one. You know what I meant, dummy.

I loved her smile.
I pointed beneath the rim and showed her where to stand.
We matched each other's buckets until we got to the elbow.
Then, I missed.
I looked down at my crooked finger.

You'll learn to work around it, Bobcat.

I hoped so. It made me so mad, I caught myself trying to
POP the knuckle with my thumb.

Don't do that. You'll mess it up again, Isis soothed.

Let's just play! I said, through gritted teeth.

Mike made his shot and so did
Isis.
They left me be-
hind.
And I never caught up.
As I watched them go 'round
the world,
I imagined me
not in it.

When it came my turn to shoot,
I HURLED it as hard as I could
sending it off the backboard and
into the bushes.

There's poison ivy in there, Isis warned.

Yeah, man, it's game off now. THANKS.

You're welcome, I spat, walking to

my basement door.

I didn't want to play again.
I wasn't that good anyway.
Maybe I could drive a semi-truck, with
my one dumb hand, like Dad did.

BASKETBALL BLUES

The Seton Varsity squad won region and went to state.
They played in RUPP ARENA, in Lexington!
Despite my stupid anger,
I went to Mike's games.
Isis told me I would get a chance
to play *there* someday.

What she really said was,
I believe in you, Levi.

And Mom was our plus one.
She wore my #42 practice jersey,
just because.

I told her I was a *spectator*.

She didn't flinch.

*You and Mike have more chemistry
than those seniors do. I came for you
AND him.*

I looked out and saw him
preparing for the tip.

Rupp was GORGEOUS.
(Not a word I use much).
But it was the truth.
Holding 24,000 people for Wildcat home games,
it was something else.

I pictured myself shaking hands with some rival,
wiping my hands religiously on my jersey,

and fiddling with my nose
like I had a booger hidden somewhere.

Why do you always touch your nose so much? Mom always asked.

If I knew, I'd TELL YOU.

Mike got the tip at half-court,
landing on the big UK logo.
I laughed when I thought about how much he wished it was the
baby blue outline of North Carolina.
But here he was, and he played like he always did—
mean and extra hungry.
It was true there wasn't the same gel between him and
the Seton Varsity squad.
He called for the ball, and they only gave him the rock
every third trip down the court.
He could EASILY score fifty on those guys, but
he wasn't getting the action.
The seniors were trying to prove a point, but really they
WEREN'T.
Shots were going BONG, WHACK, BONG, WHACK
against the rim, the backboard.

Coach Turpin yelled stuff like—
Throw it to the seven-footer!

But they went on shooting, and the team's stay in Lexington
was short.
We went home (Isis, Mom, and me) in the family
van.

Mike traveled back with the team, on the
big, yellow bus.
I wasn't happy they'd lost, because that would be the jerkiest thing
in the world.
I thought about the scouts, shaking their ink pens and jotting down
Mike's stats.

They *had* to see more than what they saw in those four quarters.

I imagined they wrote things like:
Seven-feet
Wingspan seven-three
Added weight since JV start
Good footwork
Aware of skip passes
Vocal to teammates
Didn't see enough passes
High basketball IQ
Great attitude in team huddles
Attacks the rim well
Could've gone for fifty

ESPN RECRUITING

Mike told me they were ALREADY forming lists.

Lists for what?

You know how they do?

No. Who?

Scouts, he said, like that explained it.

I gave him my best 'Help Me Out' look.

They make lists like years in advance.

For college?

YEARS in advance.

I laughed.

We'll just be in ninth grade.

I know. They get giddy or something. What class would that be, Bobcat? 20 . . . ?

2023.

Mike chuckled.

That's crazy, I said.

Bobcat, I might have a full beard by then.

I might have a mustache, too, you think?

If you keep eating your Wheaties.

He reached in like he was trying to
touch my lip.

Get a room you noobs, Isis said.

She took the ball and started dribbling
around my goal.

What're you doing this summer, Bobcat?

Helping Dad with his truck . . . it's getting pretty old.

The semi sat over in the grass. He was home for a few
days.

*Isis, are you gonna find a new man in
Guatemala?*

It's a MISSION trip, Mike, she said, dribbling better than
Ozzie could.

But it's like the WHOLE summer.

It's just a month.

I looked at her, wondering if that could happen.

I got all the man I want right here, she laughed, picking up
the ball and staring at me.

And you'll be off at AAU camps, Mike, I said.

Coach Turpin thinks it'll do me good.

Coach Turpin. What about Coach coach? I asked.

What about him?

Will you ever be playing JV again?

But I knew the answer before he said
ANYTHING.
He was Varsity material now.
It would be dumb for him to risk getting
hurt.

You gotta think about UK, I said.

No way, Bobcat. You know I'm headed south.

Isis said, *It IS a prettier blue.*

I gave her a cold stare, put my head phones on.

What're you listening to, bruh?

Mike took my ear bud out, put it in his ear.

It's Royal Blood.

He listened for a second and took the head phone
out.

You white boys gotta listen to something with a little more groove.

I laughed at him.

Sure sure.

I MEAN it. You have to work on THAT playlist.

What's wrong with 'Figure it out'?

Figure what out?

That's the name of the song.

They can't figure it out for you, he joked.

Isis cracked up.

I put the music back on and ignored
both of them.

REST

Summer was brutal   for me.
Isis went somewhere   south.
Mike wanted to go south,   too.
I didn't see anything wrong with   Seton.
Dad said, *Hand me the wrench* about fifty times   straight.
Mom picked strawberries and made   more jam.
She asked me how I was doing, and I   shrugged.
I didn't know how to answer   THAT.

Well, just rest a   *little bit.*

What else can I   *do?*

Help your dad, I hear him rattling with something   *else.*

He does most of it   *himself.*

He needs your eyes, Levi. Otherwise he might hurt   *himself.*

REPAIRED

I wiggled my finger, flexed it,
TRIED to palm the ball.

It hurt, but the crooked digit
OBEYED.

Mike was back from AAU.
FINALLY.

He'd called to say, *Let's run some laps at the park.*

I hated running.

But he was BACK.

It was like Christmas morning.

If he'd wanted to throw rocks at a Seton stop sign,
I'd said, *How big do you want the rocks, #23?*

I put on my stiff, stale Nikes and pulled the laces
TIGHT.

I heard the knock on my front door.

Come in, honey, Mom's voice called.

Mike fist-bumped me, and it was as good as a
hug.

You ready?

Okay, I thought. We're skipping AAU talks altogether.

We got in the van, and Mom hauled us to the
park.

I'll just park over here in the shade, she said, pointing
to a shelter house.

How many laps you wanna do?

Mike stroked the mustache, *Five sounds good. You ready?*

A lap is a mile. That's FIVE miles! I blurted.

It'll separate the men from the boys, he said, kicking my right shoe.

Good.

We took off at a pace I knew I couldn't keep, and he actually jogged backwards at times, around
the abandoned track.

It felt like a million degrees.

BECAUSE IT WAS.

It was late July in southern Kentucky.

Mike noticed me huffing, and he jogged in place, while I felt tunnel vision
taking over.

The TV screen of my vision was going dark.

Can you make it through this third lap?

I . . . will . . . do . . . it, man. If it kills me.

That's the spirit, Bobcat!

He smacked me on the back, and I don't remember
the rest.

We rounded the last corner, and the beige van sitting under a tree look like
heaven.

Mom had water in the cooler.

Mike talked to Mom, barely winded.

I leaned against the metal frame and felt my lunch
sloshing around my insides.

GHOST

Willie brought the ball up in practice.
He tossed it to Ozzie.
Ozzie skipped the ball over to me. I looked inside and felt the gap of our missing
center.
The play was meant to be ran inside, but it couldn't be
without Mike.
Instead, I flung the ball to our power forward, Cade.
He looked at the ball like he couldn't believe it went to him.
Coach blew the whistle and wanted to know what I was doing.

The ball was SUPPOSED to go inside, son. Snap out of it! Coach barked.

I didn't care. The team didn't feel whole
anymore.

SWIMMING

The call came to the house, and I stopped playing a board game with Isis.

I bet that's Mike, I said, getting up, and dusting my hands of another lost game.

Mom mumbled in the kitchen, telling someone to speak LOUDER.
She said my name, and I asked who it was.
Coach's voice croaked like a bullfrog's right into my ear.
It's me, Levi . . . It's Coach.

I found it hard to place the voice outside of the gym.

The reason I'm calling is . . . well, I wanted to let you know there's been an ACCIDENT.

Isis got up from the game and came over to me.

I cradled the phone in my hand.

I heard the croak sounds mumbling through the receiver.
Mike was swimming at the lake . . .

(Mike didn't swim . . . EVER.)

He was goofing around with some of the Varsity . . .

(Mike couldn't swim. He'd told me EVERY time I mentioned Kentucky Lake.)

He went UNDER, son. And, he didn't come up . . .

Where is he, then?

They're looking for him right now . . .
As soon as I know something, I'll let you know, okay?

We were supposed to go to DQ later, I said to Isis and Mom, more than to the phone.

Then, I dropped it and hugged Isis.

The house felt empty and TOO big.

Mom was crying into her shirtsleeve.

I stared at the board game.

My brain couldn't think of ANYTHING except DQ milkshakes.

The lake was just ten minutes away,

but it felt like

a whole different planet.

SETON HERALD

Mike Mulaney, 14, of Seton, drowned on Friday, July 20th, 2018.

Mike was born in Seton on April 5, 2004. He is survived by his father, Daunte Mulaney of Seton.

Mike was a devoted son—
a friend to everyone he met.

He played basketball and
was a stalwart talent for the Seton Lions—leading them to the Kentucky state tournament
for the first time in over thirty years.

Mike was a fun-loving, tender boy and
will be supremely missed.

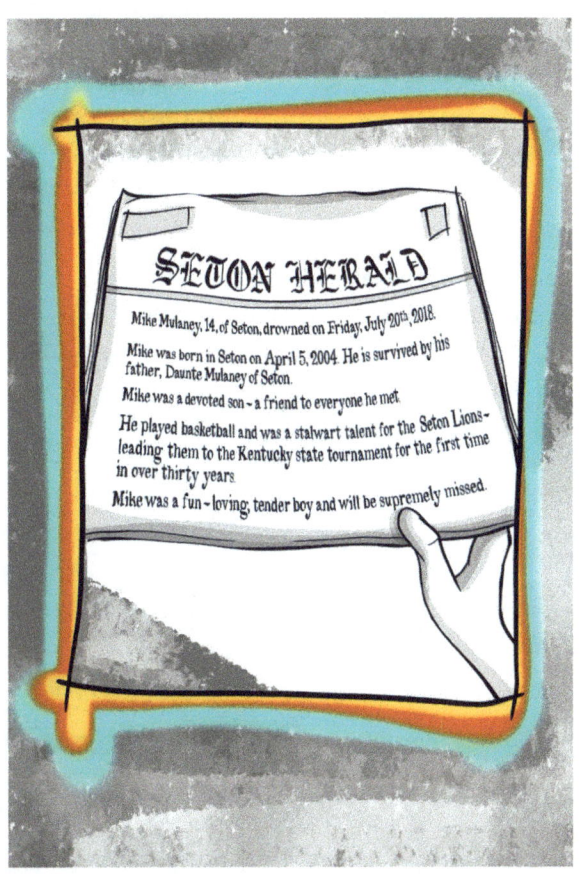

STALWART

I looked it up on my phone, the word
stalwart.

Mike was that AND
all those other things the paper said.
He WAS devoted, fun-loving, and talented.

And SO much more . . .

He was my:

stubborn
passionate
best friend
the coolest dude
confident
cocky
and prepared

always . . .

MEMORIAL

Mr. Mulaney laid flowers inside the open casket.
Mike rested on the cushioned coffin below.
It was Mike but not really.
He was cold, bluish.
His brown skin looked polished, glossy even.
His mustache didn't move, and I kept waiting for him to
reach up, say, *Get me out of here, Bobcat!*

But this wasn't a joke.
(Mike's eyes were closed.)

There were people in the Seton gym crying and crying.
I heard someone wail beside me on the bleachers.
Isis gripped my hand, and I kept staring at midcourt.

The team sat on the front row with Coach—
everyone but ME.
Cade kept looking back into the crowd
and eventually found me.

I didn't wave or nod.
The principal asked for a moment of silence.

I didn't pray.
I didn't think God would hear me,
or, anyone else.

The service ended, and the pallbearers
(Mike's family)
went up and stood
at the four corners
of the box.

PERSEVERANCE

The principal told me I showed
perseverance.

He asked me to speak into the school intercom,
say something Mike would say.

Like what?

You knew him better than anyone.

I pushed the intercom button, my finger shaking, then released it.

Go ahead, Levi.

I couldn't think of a thing.
Mike was gone.
I wouldn't see him EVER AGAIN.
Tears came to my eyes, and I wanted to
RUN home.

Take your time. What would he say, if he was here right now?

I looked around the principal's crummy space and stared at the pictures
on the wall.
There were fake, motivational frames saying things like:
Goals: You can do it, and *Just believe in yourself.*

I thought of Mike's laugh and heard it strongly inside my head.
I pushed the button again and smiled.
The words were there.

Listen up, Lions, I said in my best Mike voice. *This is for you.*

THE CURRENT GAME OF BASKETBALL

Mike stands under the ten-foot goal
CALLING for the ball with his 7'3" wingspan.

BALL BALL BALLLLL

I fake an entry pass, and then FEED it
to him.

He catches the ball and squares his back to the basket.
Two defenders collapse on him.
He palms the ball in one big hand.
Then, he brings the ball around to face the D.

Coach shouts for everyone to *CLEAR OUT!*

Mike pump fakes the ball and one defender
bites, jumping in the air, leaving his feet.
Mike bounces it once off the floor.
He drop steps the other player and looks out at me
on the wing.

I call, MIKE, and he dishes it to me on the wing.

I catch it, faking a shot. The defender flies past me.
I square up to shoot the J but don't.

Instead, I no-look pass it back inside, and Mike
goes up UP UPPPP,

and he takes the ball

home SWEET home.

www.ingramcontent.com/pod-product-compliance
Lightning Source LLC
Chambersburg PA
CBHW071437160426
43195CB00013B/1940